YARN

Peter Dent

Leafe Press

Published by Leafe Press
Nottingham, England.
www.leafepresspoetry.com

Copyright © Peter Dent, 2021. All rights reserved.

Cover photograph: "A glove made of "plarn", "plastic yarn", yarn made from plastic bags" by Dianakc
CC BY-SA 4.0 <https://creativecommons.org/licenses/by-sa/4.0>, via Wikimedia Commons
© Copyright DianaKC and licensed for reuse under Creative Commons Licence.

ISBN: 978-1-9999451-1-4

CONTENTS

AT LEAST ONE YARN'S DIED THE DEATH, 7
A YARN FOUND WANTING, 8
ONE YARN TO ANOTHER, 9
THE TRUE HEFT OF A YARN, 10
EDUCATION AND TRAINING (A YARN), 11
GETTING YOUR YARN IN, 12
A RIB-CRACKING YARN FOR WOULD-BE EXHIBITORS, 13
LOST YARNS LOOKING FOR THEIR WORDS, 14
TELL ME ANOTHER, 15
WATCHING YARNS FROM BEHIND THE SOFA, 16
EXTRA-RURAL YARNS, 17
OPTIMISM AND THE YARN (OR KINDLINESS FOR LATE BEGINNERS), 18
CONSISTENCY IN A YARN IS NOT NECESSARILY A RECOMMENDATION, 19
YARNS WILL TALK TO THEMSELVES, 20
YARN WARP, 21
IF IT'S DEATHGRIND I CAN'T MAKE IT WORK (SAD YARN), 22
FITFUL AND FUGACIOUS YARNS, 23
WINNING YARN, 24
PREMIER YARN ONCE REMOVED, 25
QUICK YARN, 26
DISPENSING WITH A YARN, 27
THIS YARN NOT THAT YARN, 28
YARNS FAST AND LOOSE, 29
YARN FOR YARN, 30
YARNS AFTER DARK, 31
SOME YARNS BEST FORGOTTEN, 32
A YARN ONCE THOUGHT DEAD, 33
ONE YARN TOO MANY, 34
SPLITTING A YARN, 35
WONDERING ABOUT YARNS IN A PARALLEL UNIVERSE CAN TAKE YEARS OFF YOUR LIFE, 36
AN EMINENTLY REASONABLE YARN, 37

OVERLIT YARN, 38
INSTEAD OF A YARN, 39
YARN TO END ALL YARNS, 40
YARNS IN FULL RETREAT, 41
HANGING A YARN OUT TO DRY, 42
COMMERCIAL YARN, 43
YARN AT THE POINT OF DISCLOSURE, 44
COMPULSIVE-CREATIVE YARNS REQUIRING HELP, 45
SEASONING A YARN, 46
UPSETTING A YARN, 47
YARNS OF NIL CONSEQUENCE, 48
TWO-THIRDS OF A REVELATORY YARN, 49
IT DOESN'T TAKE MUCH FOR A YARN, 50
CARNIVAL TIME: AN EMBROIDERED YARN, 51
ECONOMICAL YARN, 52
SOME YARNS HAVE STORIES OF THEIR OWN, 53
QUESTIONABLE YARN, 54
A YARN AND A GOOD HALF, 55
THE YARN OF BEYOND, 56
UNREPEATABLE YARNS, 57
THE LIMITS OF A YARN, 58
PERIOD YARN, 59
ONE YARN IS NEVER ENOUGH ONE MORE CAN
      BE MURDER, 60
A YARN FOR TODAY, 61
UNSPECIFIED YARNS OF THE MOMENT, 62
RUNNING UP A YARN, 63
THE ONE AFTER THE ONE BEFORE, 64
YARN OF A DESERT FATHER (AFTER TINARIWEN), 65
HALF A YARN HALF A HEART (AT THE EQUINOX), 66
YARN WITH BLACK AND MAROON, 67

*How simple everything would have been
If we had never opened the door.*

Ian Robinson (in: 'The Invention of Morning',
Redbeck Press, 1997)

AT LEAST ONE YARN'S DIED THE DEATH

The school closed long ago – I can still hear the bell. The pastry-maker and the corner shop thought better of it and retired to tend dahlias – I see them gesticulating at pesky pigeons which if they're not parodying themselves are lost in meditation: only they know how they're doing. I'd say it matters that the 20th Century's lost its way here – battles between critics and surrealism no longer have an edge. I wouldn't say I'm a zealot – I'm not for re-introducing the egos of yesteryear or the masterminds of political persuasion but it will mean more than walking the dog. Students are now topographically challenged – employment is not for heading west. Where the sun sets observe the steady depletion of futures. Playgrounds fly only branded kites. It's a miracle my eyes have any idea what they're seeing.

A YARN FOUND WANTING

The carnival was only too obviously over; footsteps heard on the stairs belonged bizarrely to none of us. If we'd cared to we could have called in Old Moore (current edition). That didn't happen – the girl with the lazy eye felt like sleeping the sleep of the dead but you can't really can you? Bearing true witness is to some if not to me an occupational hazard. The rising of the sun brought warmth and apathy – and with that she ran for the bus. What some thought 'not of this world' was nothing more than an apple tree tapping at the window. Nothing I'd created was stolen or interfered with or spoiled. Security advised to 'proceed with caution' – the 'unconscious' likewise. The job of the living unfailingly is 'to be un-dead'.

ONE YARN TO ANOTHER

I am overwhelmingly anxious – checkpoints in the big city are getting me down. Less enthralled than I once was I comb the area for indications of superficial damage and lethal intent. It reminds me of the war. My time spent watching trams die out and people omitting to wear trilbies. To say money isn't an incentive doesn't mean money is without consequence. I feel words pressing in on all sides. Do you? Do you treat leafy areas with more care than scruffy side-streets? There have to be compromises when our betters demand it – by the light of a string of streetlights today will find its way home. My score I believe is carefully conducted by the mind I've attached to it. Reasons are set out (overleaf) on how to be alive – or at the least enjoying Autumn. I don't mind what you do: being words only you can always listen to their song.

THE TRUE HEFT OF A YARN

Ice walls do not an igloo make. Words to see through do as well. Claustrophobia comes when you can't see the hand before you and the dagger's red. A vantage point has provisos concerning the weather. Indoors noticeably shaken but conspiratorially without compass. They are ready to give succour even as they collapse tenses or dash hopes; between us there is a choice of irregular militias and villains wanting blood. I refuse to take up arms against the infinite.

EDUCATION AND TRAINING (A YARN)

The new intake had known 'smarter schools' – they made no bones. (In the middle of a middling career or at the close I can always trounce such claims. Staffrooms practised in disorder see no takers when it comes to plugging a distaste for cash.) Professional means pragmatic; ice means water. A fall in profits means you cut Act 5. She considered it an upheaval in kind – collapsed clouds likely to originate in the director's mind as in a Book of Hours where peasants work fields to the ground. She 'acted' superbly: I'd say she gave it some. Seniors predictably played it and the rest strictly for laughs which some thought hollow – I bought into it all.

GETTING YOUR YARN IN

Cross-examinations do as much for mental well-being as buttercups do for a cow with dairy difficulties. I can't handle bright lights and when I'm stretched I get instant cramp. How tolerant and understanding is the questioner is either a known unknown – perhaps a good one for cocking a snoop or mocking a lisping brief – or it's another fine mess I've got into and likely as not won't get out of short of sky-blue intervention. Dialogue it isn't. The one to do me today has a history of bad breath and instability. I'm at the place where actuality goes AWOL.

A RIB-CRACKING YARN FOR WOULD-BE EXHIBITORS

Visually impaired Members in a full face-off. Critics show up unexpectedly after the event but before the handouts. Your suspicions raised by a too carefully nuanced explanation. Do I hold with forcing no longer young initiates to sleep rough? Someone will sour the footnotes – wives infuriate at Triple A. Until that racket overhead soaks up what you say what I say won't so much count as troll the past. Dystopia just now is tacking; mast-heads fly black pennants to uncommon effect. Disquisitions on Redundant Art see new curators out of a job.

LOST YARNS LOOKING FOR THEIR WORDS

Everyone come Halloween talks about afterwards and how light changes everything.   You could try adding drama and whatever it is that's different again about her eyes.   Image-projection .... the sound of music .... I imagine it all and more without thinking.   Gale-force wings take some beating: the plans I pre-loaded get a lift and speak for themselves.   I'm for saying things *you* shouldn't copy without good advice. From a decade of doing nothing to one spent twirling compasses I've always needed reassurance.   Is my ghost okay?

TELL ME ANOTHER

My left eye can see further round objects of contemplation than my right which is sluggish and not to be trusted.   You wonder – I do – a lot about philosophers about politicians there is little more to be said.   Nights of the full moon even m'lud is said to inspect the backs of his hands.   Keeping a goodly range of pictures and words in mind can take you into territories that no wight can sneeze at.   Once upon a time I had a den in the woods where I rehashed worlds of 'might be'.   Planning would instantly proscribe.   Thus I painted a whopping series of pictures 'after the fact' which was described as 'prodigiously off beam'.   I can tell you from a position of trust I've seen too much of what is.   My telescope and its little yellow manual are good for a read.

WATCHING YARNS FROM BEHIND THE SOFA

If you're hereabouts in a fortnight or so watch out for fog. Michaelmas pinks and blues loll about – worrying themselves half to death. Almost. At present I've not had a lot to do so I've taken to self-examination. Something in the salivary glands may be going on – some chemical insubordination or other. I was not born yesterday. It was longer ago than that I found myself transported. If like me you're used to adverse reactions it's not so easy to go downhill at the thought of it. Stones further up the beach are going slimy. I might be anyone by Xmas.

EXTRA-RURAL YARNS

The world's as easy as pie if you know your ingredients.　But if you can't trust the baker who can you?　I could spend more time on manoeuvres than the average commando knows how to.　(My thanks to M. Messiaen and messages from the birds.) Inspirational or what I am up by 6 bushy-tailed with my daily porridge thicker and creamier than before – even before the world I invented wakes up.　Reasons exist you can go into – I still find myself held back.　We are more than we eat – we are.

OPTIMISM AND THE YARN (OR KINDLINESS FOR LATE BEGINNERS)

Till then it had been a quite forgettable life – the whole show resting in the hands of therapists and do-gooders of every description. A session with one gave 6 weeks of wherewithal. I'd then move on to another – that's how it worked. Life semi-tolerable but it's what came next that fixed me. Enrolling at a local theatre-school I learned the value of urban underbellies & shady joints: terrific when trying to get out of yourself. Tutors it is fair to say were heartfelt about getting a cure whereas I twice ran amok – not paying fees kicking over refectory tables and generally demanding more attention than I was due which was more than average. As happens of course I settled the score (and in) – surprising various of the semi-cloned dismal 1st years I'd used to help me pull up my socks and see to the laces. As a thank you I'd show off my paces. It's been a memorable life: being on stage *all* the time rather than just some. They say I've been acting up ever since not that you'd know?

CONSISTENCY IN A YARN IS NOT NECESSARILY A RECOMMENDATION

Is it I think too much when entering orchards of disbelief or poetry known to reject the tried and trusted? I was always one for consulting old maps – checking topography and soil type. More than once finding myself bogged down in detail. A 'golden treasury' of experimentation out to defy both you and the subject matter is clearly your go-to resource. I hear the fruit on the tree is now ripe and juicy. Critics claim it offers the degree of insolence you normally associate with loftier canons in the field. No doubt about it – this is a vintage lauded in capital and regions alike. Experience tells you how just a touch of acid will add immeasurably to the sweetness though I can't help but feel all is not well overall. I'd be a lot happier if 'key features' there proved wrong – but next time round send me into raptures. Don't lead me by the nose. I can sniff out for myself that mix of exuberance and stylish restraint. I am desperate to swear.

YARNS WILL TALK TO THEMSELVES

Between us and the promotion there's a pause to make good use of. I'll scrape my boots I say I'll run a comb through my hair she says the yarn says nothing no matter how eloquently the land lies. I wanted to talk about St Anthony. A lighthouse to read your life by. Are there – yes there are – better things worth reading? I know of the storms they came from. There are a couple on the shelf you can shake the dust from.

YARN WARP

Can our economy not own its own identity?　When the U.S. sneezes aren't we all on the wagon: my comic spirit is reckoning on time curving back big time and running us down?　I can't possibly say .... but malicious masters will do anybody over (the hopes and fears of monsters can take ages to be done with; even then they may not). Thus liberty.　A fantasy of fact-chewing joy; cross-party myth-making targeting the poor; getting under the skin. I'm a latch-key liberal independent and a pro-future sky-diver with an early-onset appetite for even slower slow-cooking.　I'm a multi-bit fact-fake deviant after my tea.

IF IT'S DEATHGRIND I CAN'T MAKE IT WORK (SAD YARN)

But it didn't stand a chance. The area round here is nothing if not 'industrial'. You hear them beating metal all night long – somehow I sleep through it but I've had years to learn how. A brighter economy they promised: clean rivers a future and who remembers how many million more trees. If you don't shake to music they'll take you in says Duncan – turn you from something you've learned to deal with into memories of nothing but the past. I'm moving on – the underground here's too bright.

FITFUL AND FUGACIOUS YARNS

Some habits die away quite naturally leaving nothing but the faintest shadow.   My tins of grapefruit chunks in juice came from 'Swaziland' (Eswatini now) with lions and hippos and more.   Amazing how much you can pack in – but I can't be without it – in fact I've not had it for months.   Shortages like your lover on a sabbatical you know not where are cause for almighty distraction e.g. the clothes you put on the state of your hair even whether to turn right or left leaving home. In the mouth its impact was that of a sizeable explosion. If you're that much under the weather you'll open the can with your teeth ignoring the consequences!   Lions bite too? Joking aside I'm not so impatient now but she'll be back in a hurry if she knows what's good: all this is for putting to bed.

WINNING YARN

To say it means something is something – I did my level best coming out without blood on the walls and ceiling which is metaphorically everything.　At a very young age I was told I'd be tested – they weren't far wrong.　Ordinary as life is for most an ambiguity here and a redaction there do a lot for the low in spirits.　Anonymous 'letter-writers' can bring truth to a fair old pitch when their tongue's in their cheek and a dirge turns jaunty.　Think New Orleans funerals of old or Beauty & the Beast on ice; in my dotage 2:1 felt like I'd hit a groove. Of course they meant it.　What I didn't feel was the scratch.

PREMIER YARN ONCE REMOVED

Here isn't the place: remarkably quick decisions and disturbed
ground remember you even when time won't.   In fact
you're lucky to behold the damage.   Having an input
when sessions come to a halt is like having your own private
tutorial.   It's observable *that* particular well-tended garden
never was.   The fact we're now speaking the same language
means I can open my green eyes and ignore the contours of
the past.   It's every bit like a dog let out in the morning sun
or a goods train slamming on its brakes.   These days
I am inclined not to ask what else equally arouses and
repels?   It may well be I'll argue – but then I'll happily forget.

QUICK YARN

You couldn't make it up (if you even wanted to) this jam-packed disorderly house I walked out of unaided? Two young women slumped up against a half-collapsed cardboard box (of hard to credit dimensions) could give you cause to think this world's ready for the chop – I'll stop and let you imagine the rest. A near-capacity audience it isn't but be friendly – shove up – we can all squeeze in.

DISPENSING WITH A YARN

B Company had the knack of knowing an officer from a gooseberry bush *after* the event.   Showing 1st class opting-out skills when it came to rapid bilingual argument.   Rifles and battering rams spectacles on a post.   Lost telegrams unlooked for rotting in the swamp ....   Who came for this?   Betterment in such conditions pulls in a fearful audience – invariably when the sun shines.   The fact is doves read between broken lines: how many are we?   Peace at any price?   Who decides what to salute (obedience doesn't come cheap) – who'll dig us out?

THIS YARN NOT THAT YARN

If you can't finish chapters with some nonsense about St Elmo's fire explain how it is we're back to largely discredited rainbows?   It isn't the sky's the limit it's that recovery is perennially less than permanent.   The next time I walk on water – see Dead Sea and anything else you can stick a pin in – see that I get a wide berth: one with know-how.   I never did want for imagination – I *do* want an all-weather Cornish lugger and two hands to haul me aboard.   At least.   A modicum of sense.

YARNS FAST AND LOOSE

It had nothing to do with me.   Even so it was reported widely:
tenants victimising passers-by hanging out of windows
and going for slapstick opportunities.   This sense of humour
comes dialogue-free the way ghosts go quiet after the
event.   As a release from emptying buckets on unsuspecting
heads they pluck feathers from hens to create blizzards.
Visits from your gas engineer leave nothing to chance when
finding fault – games resorted to amount to anything
from a slap in the face of creation to snapping off a radiator
valve head.   The code behind the code he alludes to
is hardly a code and he knows it.   Falling over a trailing hose
is what a yarn does when it's scoffing at life.   Gases
don't laugh any more than poems know how to leave off but
do.   Attic windows spend days watching whole skeins
of geese flying in – but if this is a game (guess what) I'm out.

YARN FOR YARN

You can't beat it. Even when asked officials say nothing. A black cat not a black-and-white cat not a brindle. Black as a museum with a power cut. Other things: a dead sky and a squeaky wheelbarrow. The possibility of a publisher for a big book I've still not written. What do you do? Immediacy. Gripping. Like a certain power tool I'm not free to mention. As much as *they* might do so easily and straight away won't. Worlds hard to share. We're on the same page and holding.

YARNS AFTER DARK

This side of the lighthouse there is nothing to concern.   The same can't be said about the ha-ha which has been caught up in a surprise flood from two nearby streams.   Lights on the water can't be confused with daybreak no matter how much we try.   In places of refuge and a holiday camp not so many miles from here the Karaoke Spot is the place to be.   People laughing or looking dazed career from one side of the room to the other.   A rocking horse in the corner gears up for a couple of would-be jockeys its paint peeling as never before. Interrogation as a way to elicit answers spends too much of its time in the dark.   Weather here is best left unremarked. I'll be entirely honest with you when I say I don't know the song they are singing (as if they know they can't be stopped).

SOME YARNS BEST FORGOTTEN

One 30-minute episode of a play in 2 parts barely gets you off the ground depending hugely on the subtleties of weather of the sort we've been having haven't we?   The starting point for thinking didn't arrive till after I'd made coffee and spilt it – I'm that accomplished!   I laughed only to be told shh because one way or other a play without characters you can handle (if only at arm's length) demands you make them up.   I told myself I'd seen 'human remains' in the museum I'd rather chat to.   No answer received other than that my feelings didn't count.   An appraisal will doubtless be awaiting bye and bye saying how critical it is I make myself scarce.   We shall have to see?

A YARN ONCE THOUGHT DEAD

In forgotten suburbs even the moon turns rusty. The key to survival and not advancement is secured via a double-turn lock. Within shouting distance we have zones of self-prediction and scallywags smashing lamps while the devil suffers nightlong for the taste of her lips. Scattering libations people of the sunny south risk losing face even as they empty their enormous lungs. I don't know which of the current crop of racketeers is for moving us into houses of despair? I see plenty; they see what they want you to and get on with it. The Governor on his 4th single whisky revels in the prime delights of loaded dice.

ONE YARN TOO MANY

3 days of on/off rain seem like forever. Hedge sparrows are cowering under the azalea and doing their best to look nondescript – that or making a smart move in the department of disguise. After all they are on the ground and therefore at risk. 'Forever' produces something a lot like compound interest but 3 days – if they're anything – show nothing in the way of profit; makeshift money or money on paper won't lift my spirits – that's evident to any house sparrow wet or dry. The last love letter I received arrived in a colossal downpour. However much blame I took on there was a stubborn trickle.

SPLITTING A YARN

Tell nobody what you don't know.   Amaze me with your multivalent plain and peculiar talents.   Remember my New Hudson amaranth upright?   It got me around – if what happened later's lost in mystery.   It visited heaven before I found others – innocence is a wonderful thing.   I take it as a gift I can respect it not exactly worship it even try to forget it but that's the difference between one quality yarn and another that seems its equal but isn't until it's over.   I love the fact angels are still at my side (they don't wake me up till Christmas).   Embarrassed is hardly word of the day.   Between me and the lamp post half a glass of light.

WONDERING ABOUT YARNS IN A PARALLEL UNIVERSE CAN TAKE YEARS OFF YOUR LIFE

The ingredients for a good pie defy the demands of logic when applied to taste – I've made a hash of porridge and what I can say about blackberry and almond tart will have you blanch. Self-parody (by definition a fool's game) if you were assigned bundles of fatuity and futility at birth. I tell myself to observe due diligence in the execution of public duties then come home-time blaze away like that gunner (RAF) who didn't just miss the target by miles – he thought cleaning up was the job of rookies not his. Copy no-one was my mantra until I'd tasted the best of what is and discovered 'provenance'. It's safe I think to confirm there are things you do and definitely do not do on your deathbed. Alfred had a thing about cakes.

AN EMINENTLY REASONABLE YARN

Throughout the noughties any number of local star-systems moved away leaving nothing astronomical to chance.
Colours and numbers ps and qs what was and wasn't in the ascendant and whatever else grew at a furious pace.　Only dyed hair and spectacular outfits allowed if you wanted to get in.　However disastrous my attempts 'to care' I knew I'd as much chance as a goth of getting home without looks!
Habitual interference in the log meant you shied away from matters of process and gave inanimate objects names.
As if the death of a planet or the private life of ions could change anyone's luck.　Big numbers don't stop at nothing.

OVERLIT YARN

Columns of white onyx bronzed bodies laughter every night set to music and whatever the dream. Compositional weakness is tantamount to disaster: for every sky to fall in there's something possibly sacramental in the air. Do I remember how it was? I like to think so. I have lines that reek of abject panic and delirium – and never mind the lyric which the lady depends on for 'life'. Ancient elusive scenes – even as we act them filling in the blanks. Guesswork is now a god. We play the play and serve. Facts vanish in clouds of light.

INSTEAD OF A YARN

Producing virtuoso design glitches and inspiring an outburst of
emotion is a key requirement.   Action guaranteed if the
demand for bodies is approved and some witch or other
doesn't mind burning.   Repeat twice a day – Wednesday and
Saturday – to packed audiences.   If only you can deliver
a palette consisting of no more than four colours.   Mixing in
helps inspire unity in the ensemble.   The longer you fit
our frame the more explosive the audience.   Try not to bang
your head on the glass or let mistresses off the hook at a
time of gross personal need: we all need a home don't we
for a background?   Screams – a deadly flight across rooftops!

YARN TO END ALL YARNS

It's more than something of an exaggeration to say that ending a sentence left him grief-stricken – stunned into submission. He was he thought ready at all times to compromise and chop a tree trunk into more manageable portions. The fire burned merrily no matter what the incentive not to without ever going out like a light. Is it a weird sort of simplification to say that of late he'd begun wondering about the probity of collapsed language – the other side of the copper coin and which he likened to a tiger pacing back and forth about its business which only he/she had any reliable knowledge of to all intents and purposes fending for itself?   It's as we know a cruel world we confront (the best way we can) speaking our mind as/when asked to.   And that being the case is there room for error or misunderstanding? Letting a caged tiger free to make its own decisions is no doubt the more acceptable approach but there are as many ways to swing a cat as chances to think twice twice.   If he couldn't quite put it into words he didn't seem to mind which approach to plump for: crushing and stretching are two halves of the same persuasion. The Science of Real Indecision sees him tossing a coin.

YARNS IN FULL RETREAT

Did she really arrive from a village with church and steeple – a stream with duckweed?   Did I really climb over the college railings and help myself to bluebells?   How often does a siren warn of an enemy approaching?   Is your house still full of things of worn-out beauty: to what extent do you consider you patch and mend?   If a job's not worth the aggravation forget it.   Asked how you're feeling everybody I know grumbles.

HANGING A YARN OUT TO DRY

Propelled into a situation *by causes* as a phrase tells you what you don't want to hear when you're after meaty explanations. To retain credibility you have to look your opponent in the eye and explode a theory that can't be broken down in a couple of minutes.   If he'd known what he was doing would he have walked out?   And being ignored at a party by the one you'd arrived with helps not one jot.   Never pull off a scab when it isn't ready is something you learn by doing and I did.   There is always something in the morning papers you can never find online.   Doubt is what dogs any unguarded sentence with a hint of weariness deadlines and near-desperation for a cup of black coffee.   Social calendars give it all up without a fight.   Maybe I've led a quiet life maybe it was the other way round?

COMMERCIAL YARN

Runs on and on and only when you think it won't stop do they entertain the idea.   Some of these ideas beggar belief.   The learning of lessons has clearly fallen by the wayside.   You can only get so much blood out of the stone in your shoe quipped a former director.   For my part I shy away from anything that sounds like repetition but now and again I fall under its spell. Clerics and Clerks of Court and any number of post-war poets for sure love regular forms.   Even a piece like this demands I first get that ringing out of my ears.   Pattern is easy to upset even when there's no planned ending – which is where we go.

YARN AT THE POINT OF DISCLOSURE

In an attempt to avoid the camera hiding behind lamp posts they pause.   Beyond the shutter is a world of trial and error where voices and petrol bombs rack up ruin.   I can learn too much from a young person's next to last breath.   I can re-rehearse my own.   Everlasting days.   Volume on the up.

COMPULSIVE-CREATIVE YARNS REQUIRING HELP

I once was creative since when I've operated to a fixed timetable. My best albums were torn to shreds. Others I preferred merited no more than a mention. What I did not care for far from languishing rocketed to the top. At any given moment I will not be complacent – by the light of sanctimony I hold my breath shield my eyes and apply 1st and 2nd principles. A distillation of the centuries had I attempted it next would have been considered criminal – something ripped out of another's rulebook. Not at all welcomed by the owner later not even by me. Humanity itself (can I make such a judgment?) deserves better. If I'm surviving (various – not every department) it's because I have rearranged my locker. According to what's on my shelves; hanging by the skin of my (fast depleting) teeth; or half out the door I'm seeking alliance with simply what at any given time and in any place actually IS. There said someone that wasn't so bad was it? I told her right away I had no idea she cared – still if she wanted to she was a free woman. Thus I allowed myself to be 'actioned' i.e. put on the contemporary rack and cranked (whatever the word or expression is). The sounds I make are not for a minute me but seriously do I care? Everything in life is ready to be tweaked. Everything like indecision in love to closing both eyes when crossing the road has paid off.

SEASONING A YARN

I exercise to a set routine. I wake as and when the birds do and go out running – watching the leaves fall loving hearing them crunch underfoot. There's a certain peace to be had in the land of lifestyles and exotic doings. Birds overhead I submit to a sweet interrogation. Forgive them I remember the pastor saying they're doing what they must. So I squat and stretch and urge myself into positions none would have thought possible in this age of prostration. I put myself in the hands of a script tucked in my sock for all contingencies. Man in a hurry to be known – to himself and those he loves.

UPSETTING A YARN

So I headed off into the ether with you and a couple of hastily assembled constructions.   I was fortunate in more ways than one: I had a girl to hold hands with and a devil of a job to hold her.   My son talked of trickery with a skate-board – I took off on the subject of 'designer design faults'.   The new Swedish thriller was indeed unsolvable.   The protagonist had much in common with myself nay everyman but I can honestly say the body on page 14 described in a sonnet written by the killer at the very scene and artificially stained by the printer left more distress than something in real life.   But 'real life' set out in a novel won't let you browse minds.   I had to consult my own.   By nightfall we were back where we began.   By the look of it.

YARNS OF NIL CONSEQUENCE

Unless she'd not as I'd thought become *the* pivotal moment in my book I'd have dreamed up a signal other – amber being my perennial state of mind I'm poised to resume my investigations into the unknown. We saw the circus and were not impressed with ourselves; we flew with geese (cameras attached) over ice-cold waters; we chatted with the best of an untidy bunch of reprobates about which rule to trash next. I saw myself cringe and her fly off the handle. There was more in the way of recrimination – to be posted as a warning to others – than I had screen time for. The book she herself had proposed consisted more of appendices than out and out narrative; content had very nearly lost its way. If a life is everything and nothing then my words were halfway there.

TWO-THIRDS OF A REVELATORY YARN

May be disregarded.   I cannot expect myself to be clearer given the data the night and the lady of my dreams.   Fundamental apprehension's the bane of more MPs' hustings than you'd think.   Rank inconsequence will take many a fair voter from his happy home.   Preferring 2 in the bush to 1 in the hand is nothing if not some private aberration.   Sweat breaks out when I think about it and I do – much as a loving wife in a rush to defy gravity and the electorate forgets to declare her own good name.   Speak to me my friend I said of her eyes – don't dwell on loss.   Only love and art have the faintest who I am.   One or two stitches in time may lead to voter salvation.   So here's to 'belief'; to a surge in the polls – what some refer to as dismissible upswings!   A return to alternative if old-fashioned grace.

IT DOESN'T TAKE MUCH FOR A YARN

To let down an otherwise competent organization. Were the clerk as sensitive as the files he was handling the plan might have succeeded. Whistleblowers do no better. The biggest mistake I ever made (I will admit to) lay in giving credence to 'notions of certainty'. 9 trusties tasked with double-checking entrances exits and other weak points (never mind Security itself) weren't enough to cover every angle. The idiot – a quiz fanatic with a phenomenal memory inadvertently hard-wired the codes and regurgitated them out loud in his sleep – what else can a home monitor do but record? An open mind is just the job to flush facts out. Officially I don't myself need help but I do get to wonder about Free Verse and 'streams of the unconscious'. The material I have amassed is unfamiliar.

CARNIVAL TIME: AN EMBROIDERED YARN

Of the giving and bequeathing of stuff in some of these old wills there is plenty. Nowadays we can't stop feeding charity shops with cast-offs and unwanted 'free gifts'. Presently I can't see any way out of analysis without entertaining gurus mentors even the girl behind me in the queue with a delinquent child.   Surely the appeal of the past is that all of its appurtenances material and otherwise are so far out of reach as to be items of wonder?   I throw up my hands when I catch one rolling by.   Like a carnival float in full rig.   I go by example every time caution is thrown to the winds: like so. How eerie when sentences connect with others typed earlier.

ECONOMICAL YARN

I am all for contriving a little silence. Or approximations to such a 'condition'? Intractable distances in time and a love of macrame keep some of our worlds from establishing an unnatural independence. A too busy day in the workshop dog-tired with the job only half-done ensures I fail to appreciate small print with the naked eye: of all the libraries I've lived and worked in I can think of nothing worse than the sound of zealous reading. The man in the desert in the ad I can't stand's either burying something intrinsically personal or dumping a life – is that it? If I'd read those last figures from the bank satori mightn't have seemed so close. A minotaur thinks less about a ball of string and lots more about himself but doesn't every complex argument have holes in it? Peace after nights of compendious bellowing.

SOME YARNS HAVE STORIES OF THEIR OWN

Like the one about Freud and his 'friend' who sold him a pup: the chaise was all green velvet and trés agréable but the legs gave way at only the second appointment. Looking back at that yarn in particular it did invite abuse. It described multifarious attempts by writers to seduce editors and get loaded contracts at a time of economic unrest. I like things that go bang in the night or missing. Subsequently found under a cushion: weight makes all the difference to minds in turmoil. Only a mug thinks none of this applies to him – plumb loco. Metaphors like 'analogies' can make me 'feel more at home'!

Last line: a partial quote from Sigmund Freud 'New Introductory Lectures on Psychoanalysis' (1933)

QUESTIONABLE YARN

Woken by the circus in my head I'd been curating.   Silent as a witness to murder in a current paperback rustling to order only.   I might be misled by the elephant pacing about the room or MPs after blood.   Were it not for the fact I was on a trapeze you'd hardly notice the sentence structure.   As I put it to the judge (the nth time) 'not me' but was he listening!   Smirk as much as you like.   I think as I find but sentences have more in the way of 'durability' – sawdust is everywhere.

A YARN AND A GOOD HALF

There is wand-waving if you want it – there's one rabbit after another out of a hat. The gods you played cards with have turned to the FTSE and shown what happens when you play with fire. You mess with a lender at your peril – I confront a man with a knife on a well-lit street and find I'm dreaming. It's an average day and my birthdays are as volatile as a local derby. When Bill tells me it's 'all happening' I don't believe him any more than all that's ever happened is 'still out there on the corner – the same dog biting its back'! Whether it was *his* story though doesn't come into it. I've more work than I can handle. My brain takes me only so far. When mother told me – inadvertently – she had 'only two pairs of hands' I just knew it was the Golden Age pulling up outside.

THE YARN OF BEYOND

Can you – at any given minute – remember how you came to be here or why you chose to regret one ploy more than another?   However much movement there is in highflying cirrus it's as nothing compared with a walk in the park – local as well as non-local conditions apply ask any litter collector. The passing seasons add flavour as well as fact.   Today's bloomer's not a patch on the day's before: slicing differently regardless of the hand or force applied the degree of hunger or surreal fluctuations in humidity not to mention a baker's motley crew!   I'm only toying with an imagination that if it does get out (ever) it still knows where it's at.   In battle conditions real I'm a *positive* guide to life and death.   I didn't come here on a mission or a whim; it's a shame to go.

UNREPEATABLE YARNS

Wheeler-dealers adore disappointments. They can turn screenplays into family tragedy and generate more. My friends assume the worst. They rush to group therapy before discovering what precisely has gone on. Even tones sound more soothing than ill-starred attempts to dismiss the gods – which is noisy! A betting man can wear his bruises with pride send flowers to the lady and let nature take its course. Courses to cure even a minor history of abuse pull in substantial profit – especially when re-offending's in the offing. Copycats do us all a favour by poisoning the air – gods like room to breathe.

THE LIMITS OF A YARN

Speechless in a desert of malfunctioning applications deaf underwater I find time to remind myself I'm alive. It isn't every day a shark calls.   If editors were up to it according to the saints there'd be no coming home without victories. I have two or three bags – each with a hole in or the start of one.   Not yet big enough for even small items to fall through but people die who'd live to see better.   It's one story ends on schedule.   Your face being dear holds true.

PERIOD YARN

One way or another I was whatever you dared dream of – only that was on a Tuesday – by Friday you were in a different gear swearing allegiance to the Duc de Valmer asking what else you could do to establish a media outpost in the suburbs where Art suffered like a vagrant in the stocks.   You returned as I knew you would – sleeping soundly but not with your regular herbal essence.   Hard to pin down this side of the south gate – parleying for a truce which in a roundabout way paid off. Some yarns are prone to turn up in fancy dress and by twelve carry off anyone into soggy gardens of disinformation.   So was the price paid for the Claude worth begging a queen for? Nothing doing on the small screen – it was all about her.   A mattress might serve the country not (I'm reckoning) my suit.

ONE YARN IS NEVER ENOUGH ONE MORE CAN BE MURDER

Dying twice while the going was good our old school dyslexic and sometime maker of signs knew all the backroom black political arts via The Cock and Trader.   He didn't care so much for me.   I was in the other camp polishing brass and at one with another: if she made the right choice I never knew why but the votes went blue - we all guessed guess how.   He dyed his hair blonde fled the country came back for laughs. Did he recall the old school motto I wondered: (my informal translation: 'Leave now don't be rumbled later').   He did Latin for a bit in the end did time but with heavy persuasion fixed my derailleur.   'If your bike's still a pain call out Father Nicholas.'   Can't think why I think these things (oh but I do)!

A YARN FOR TODAY

Some dream of pretensions others don't.   It's in one's nature to respect the messenger or it isn't.   There's no point ringing around for clarity on a given topic or re-writing it in the form of a fable.   It is what it is.   You can't stop a bird migrating if it's set its heart on it.   Bye and bye there'll be answers able to reproduce themselves as questions we should have asked from the start.   Had I known the minutest thing about ontology half of everything else could have been shovelled into a skip.   Last night's fracas at the Duck and Friar did little for the business.   The body on the threshold possessed no ID no papers at all apart from denials in vers libre of whatever it was he stood for.   A quiet life does for all of us bye and bye.

UNSPECIFIED YARNS OF THE MOMENT

I shouldn't attempt to intervene or at least put my mind between warring parties. An amateur philosopher will say moments answer but 'you need to wait'. And if I do does it make any difference? Hearing wise owls has me sit up straight the way I'm meant to and twiddle my thumbs. I've seen shadow puppets do worse and come to no harm whatsoever. Dust settles easily for those who do not move or facilitate easy re-awakenings. Thinking a letter will put things straight or fix a wise-woman's potion is curious? If only there were different words and happier meanings. Nice thought.

RUNNING UP A YARN

An unmeasured operation is like talking to the post-lady
about what's her side of the fence.   Romanticism
to romantics has one eye closed and one eye on the self-
destruct button – not that it makes much difference
when the mail is junk but didn't the country know that?
You can time a distance as easily as open one up
between yourself and a 3rd party.   Slowly if insecurely
I'm getting a taste for moving on.   There is weight
and measure in all things.   It's my job to wake up to it:
this making of incendiary new laws.   This weeping
forever at the words she found it in her heart to employ.

THE ONE AFTER THE ONE BEFORE

It's currently a 3-line whip; the next time you exaggerate audience size or cut back expenditure on larger-than-life exercises in what *you* call 'diplomacy' I'll call it 'nest-feathering'.   Resistance movements thrive on a brilliant opening and you can do it.   Please though .... avoid comedy at all costs – there's no future in no-man's land. Spectators find modernism in whatever catches you out.

YARN OF A DESERT FATHER (AFTER TINARIWEN)

Telling me blues grew willy-nilly out of sand; and bleeding
if she ran out of similes or lost interest in goodbye.   She
runs?   Then so will I!   What else can a book do but close
when you put it down?   Echoes stop/start.   Abscond he
said leave 'points de suspension' the prize goes elsewhere!
Look it's the fact words bent different ways aren't me.   If
one blues goes away I'll sit down and write another.   He
said there's always one to be at home with.   Guitars and
men at their coldest – the hour before dawn a heart melts.

HALF A YARN HALF A HEART (AT THE EQUINOX)

Swapping manifestoes in a hurricane isn't how you do it. China's a case in point – with a wall and GNP.   If there's a body there'll be one or another kind of sonnet for it and there is.   Not mine.   Bullet points and ricochets glorious enactments of the present past with nights growing no longer than it takes a planet to burn.   Tell you what I like: miracles to make music like everyone needs it don't we?

YARN WITH BLACK AND MAROON

Deliberation 1. 'Underbranches of a hard-to-justify gravity.' My shadow makes it (with one revision after another) to light up everything – significant and otherwise – I believe I owe. Deliberation 2. This is after all a road and being on it keeps me free. Who can speak of the circumstances of my understanding? Dead fires long ago burned the memory. Deliberation 3. It is sometimes necessary to close down words too manic to fit. You'll struggle to explain why such a fire can't be put out. Remember me – this work is confidential.

Also by Peter Dent

Simple Geometry
At the Blue Table
Settlement
Unrestricted Moment
Adversaria
Handmade Equations
Overgrown Umbrellas (with Rupert Loydell)
Ghost Prophecy
Dasein and Scarecrow
Price-Fixing
With Number Plates Disguised
Limit Situations
Trickle-Down
Repertory
Tripping Daylight
Private Utopias (or 'Noises in the Head')
Retrieval Systems
Badlands of the Real
Merryweather
The First Ghost Train out of Nowhere
The Revival of the Inspectorate for Everything
Dolly's Field
The Oort Cloud: Not a Transparent Hour
Visitors' Book Rendlesham Forest: a decomposition
Harmony-in-Black: Sixty Pieces
Lucifers
The Distances of Elizabeth Bowen
Stabbing in the Dark: 20 Abstract Speculations
A Wind-Up Collider
Mutant Summers New Histories

www.ingramcontent.com/pod-product-compliance
Lightning Source LLC
Chambersburg PA
CBHW071122160426
43196CB00013B/2678